Particularly Dangerous Situation

poems

Beth Gordon

Particularly Dangerous Situation $10.00

Clare Songbirds Publishing House Poetry Series
ISBN 978-1-947653-83-2
Clare Songbirds Publishing House
Particularly Dangerous Situation© 2020 Beth Gordon

All Rights Reserved. Permission to reprint individual poems must be obtained from the author who owns the copyright.

Printed in the United States of America
FIRST EDITION

Clare Songbirds Publishing House Mission Statement:
Clare Songbirds Publishing House was established to provide a print forum for the creation of limited edition, fine art from poets and writers, both established and emerging. We strive to reignite and continue a tradition of quality, accessible literary arts to the national and international community of writers, and readers. Chapbook manuscripts are carefully chosen for their ability to propel the expansion of art and ideas in literary form. We provide an accessible way to promote the art of words in order to resonate with, and impact, readers not yet familiar with the siren song of poets and writers. Clare Songbirds Publishing House espouses a singular cultural development where poetry creates community and becomes commonplace in public places.

140 Cottage Street
Auburn, New York 13021
www.claresongbirdspub.com

Contents

Looking Away at Lambert Airport	7
Moving Day	8
Loquacious	9
Walking Catfish	10
One of Those Days	11
I Tell You I Dreamed of Reading Poems in Phoenix	12
April Sixteenth Two Thousand Seventeen	13
Goose Season	14
Singing Buddy Holly Songs with Bobby Fischer*	15
Mirror Image	16
Particularly Dangerous Situation	17
The Possibility of Journey is a Heavy Thing	18
Inspired by True Events	19
Winter Solstice	20
Dreaming in Black and Gray	21
Road Trip Redux	22
I Think You Live in Constant Fear of Tragedy	24
The Last Wife	25
Zika and Loose Change	26
I Buried My Father Twice	27
Valentine's Day	28
Christmas Eve	29
The Ministry of Loneliness	30
Alpha or Omega	31

These poems or earlier versions of these poems were first published elsewhere as follows:

After Happy Hour Review: "Loquacious"

Anti-Heroin Chic: "Moving Day," "One of Those Days," "The Ministry of Loneliness"

Calamus Journal: "The Possibility of Journal is a Heavy Thing"

Califragile: "Looking Away at Lambert Airport," "Valentine's Day"

decomP: "Particularly Dangerous Situation"

Drunk Monkeys: "Dreaming in Black and Gray," "Zika and Loose Change"

Five:2:One: "I Think You Live in Constant Fear of Tragedy"
Hunger: "I Buried My Father Twice"

Into the Void: "Singing Buddy Holly Songs with Bobby Fischer," "Christmas Day"

JUMP International Journal of Modern Poetry: "I Tell You I Dreamed of Reading Poems in Phoenix"

Menacing the Hedge: "The Last Wife"

Occulum: "Goose Season"

Outlook Springs: "Walking Catfish"

Quail Bell: "Alpha or Omega," "Winter Solstice"

Slink Chunk Press: "Mirror Image"

Suisun Valley Review: "Alpha or Omega"

Trigger Fish: "April Sixteenth Two Thousand Seventeen"

Verity La: "Inspired by True Events"

for J.D.

Looking Away at Lambert Airport

Female twins, black-haired, arm in arm, like blind newborn
werewolves, identically addicted to meth,
disembark the plane
in St. Louis, walk into our square of terminal, so craven in eye
and mouth that we collectively believe
that when the moon
blocked our planet's star for 160 seconds, fur began to sprout
between their talons, behind their knees,
spreading like poisonous
mushrooms, only to recede when cicadas stopped singing,
when sparrows fell from trees like petrified
bones, more arachnid
than mammal, they twist their cracked lips into utterings that
only the other twin can decipher,
and then only with
the aid of potions brewed from fresh anteater blood.
Unmoved by visible magic, we return one-by-one
to our screens, like sedated
vultures waiting for someone to die in front of us, bubonic
plague, rabies, salmonella, something
riddled with bullets
and primary colors that we can photograph and share with our
high school classmates whose skin we
haven't touched
in years or our online food-addiction support group as we
browse through 81 recipes for heavenly hash,
while eclipse stragglers
with souvenir tattoos and mildly damaged retinas scream
obscenities at their precocious children who
are using a gift shop
magnifying glass to aim the sun's holy rays onto unattended
babies to see if they will burst into ash.

Moving Day

While you are in Mississippi moving furniture from your child-
hood home, vacuuming cockroaches
that survived in crevices

for fifty years, giving away flowerpots and cutlery to strangers
in the right place at the right time,
driving with rum in a plastic

cup, your backseat filled with boxes of newspaper articles, una-
ble to decide which words to keep, which
to discard, the temperature

here drops twenty degrees. One year ago today we rode the
train from Chicago to St. Louis, marveled
at lush green cornfields, more

rain forest than amber waves of grain, drank wine straight
from the open bottle because we forgot
to pack cups and did not speak

of my daughters' childhood friend, murdered by heroin, found
face down eight hours after the crime.
I was drinking too much then

and now I wonder if I'm drinking enough, alone in six rooms,
day after day content with background
movie noise, my mother's voice

calling to see if my cough is dead, the manager of the local
drugstore who doesn't know whether to flirt
or be concerned that I'm buying

vodka on a cool Sunday morning, and 400 miles away with
nothing left to pack, you are in a hotel
shower, washing dirt from your pores,

beneath your fingernails, letting the water flow hotter and hotter
to rid your lungs of mold, of kudzu tears,
of weeping printer's ink.

Loquacious

She wants me to stop talking. She thinks I don't know that she wants me to stop talking. She thinks I won't smash the glass-top coffee table with my fist if she lets me talk all night. We're taking off in September, moving to Paris, if we are both still alive that is. She's dying inside and not because of a proverbial coat hanger. Internal bleeding is the least of our concerns. God is on vacation so I'm punishing myself with Adderall, enough to keep me awake seven nights in a row. It doesn't have to be Paris, it just has to be somewhere else but here. Her lipstick, the color of poisonous apples, reaches across the room, touches my soul like a modern-day talisman and I see an entirely different future, complete with black-suited men and destitute opera singers peddling their wares on the train platform. She wants me to stop talking but I have to tell her what my daughter's hair felt like in my hand after she was dead. No matter how many pints of dried blood we have seen on the sidewalk, the knowledge we have gained, the ability to tell the difference between enchanted sleep and dead, we can't get used to the idea. We will still be shocked when it's our turn. When the biopsy reveals the cancer that we have always known was there.

Walking Catfish

There is no orange in my dreams where green bottle flies
swarm and glisten, shiny sharp tornadoes, an eternal nuclear

winter as far as the soul can see, as cold as pink embalming
fluid that adds a glow to the faces of the dead. I don't search

for the sun, I don't look up, I'm on the edge of finding a cure
for cystic fibrosis. Tomato plants grow taller than my knees,

taller than the top of trees, nothing ever ripens, nothing bursts
bright juice or saturated seeds. If I were to find that distant star,

my eyes would never adjust, like coming in after a day in the
New Mexico desert, watching man's creation melt sand into

glass. I don't pretend to understand smallpox or diphtheria, the
quarantine has failed, a great white owl swims in the muddy

river waiting for migrating catfish to arrive. Ghosts without
sound, survivors of nightmares, they appear in my path, they

don't pause, don't acknowledge my presence, DNA testing is
unnecessary, we already know the results. They walk, these

unusual things, deceptive as cows, they smell the water, the
owl's talons, the fire in my lungs. They turn a frozen corner

and one-by-one they disappear, the last one turns and mutters.
Don't forget the tiger lilies. I wake to orange flowers.

One of Those Days

Our gourmet hamburgers interrupted by the phone call,
pineapple marinade, avocado and fried green
tomatoes put on hold, my best
friend's father, held captive by doctors and his oxygen-
deprived brain, gasping for vocabulary, proper
syntax for a single sentence,
I want to go home. Two seconds away from our first cocktail,
we see the day's tone shift from black-
berry pie to hospital monitors,
DNR orders, our lunch date orders the *slopper* with extra BBQ
sauce and creamy cold slaw, she tells us
about the lead wires
in her heart, first inserted at age 10, old enough so that she
would not pull at the stitches, scratch
through scarred skin
and undo the surgeons good work, young enough that she
believed for years her state of destruction
was normal. She asks us to meet
her in December and cook meals for parents of tumor-ridden
children with poor appetites and immune
systems, crumbling with fear,
enough for 30 people, she says, something thick and familiar
that can be preserved in plastic containers,
reheated and consumed at 11:00
at night when they leave the ICU not knowing what will happen
while they sleep. We navigate from
restaurant to Greek goddesses
sliced in half by helicopter blades, their eyes facing in two
different directions, and a woodland deer
taller than my house, Viking ship
bones, rotting persimmons, a wedding party raising champagne
glasses to the 30-foot eyeball. We search
overhead for the source
of buzzing, expecting a swarm of killer bees that's been
traveling here since 1974, but discover, instead,
a spidery drone, controlled
remotely by young lovers hidden between the evergreen
trees. Wind chimes
are ringing, a train cries out,
we photograph our shrinking
shadows, we sing *Bohemian Rhapsody* as a sudden storm
follows us, dead leaves in hand, to the back
booth of our favorite bar.

I Tell You I Dreamed of Reading Poems in Phoenix

Watching orange-petaled words explode like hijacked planes
over the sandstorm sky, skipping
stones across nocturnal puddles and you say *I've been dreaming
of water,* wanting your skin
to be saturated, drenched, so desperate for drowning that you
pried open the deadbolt of a prepackaged
retirement home that bloomed where nothing else can grow,
helped yourself to the shower, held
onto the safety rail and hoped the widowed owner was a deep
sleeper, bubble-wrapped in dreams
of happier endings without oncoming cars that crossed the solid
line. *I haven't bathed in days,*
I confess, a kind of self-destruction, knowing that my muse
delivers Thumbelina phrases between
water drops, I stubbornly exist in dirty frayed pajamas with only
peanut butter and cheap red wine
to nourish me inside my windowless rooms. The meteorologist
announces a deep freeze tonight
and I am shocked to hear that it's no longer July. You tell me
Christmas is 15 days away, time
for my pilgrimage into the desert, but every time I see one shoe
on the highway's edge, a single glove
or earring, I wonder if it's missed. *She woke up,* you tell me,
the widow, invited you to reflect
upon her life, perhaps a different career, licensed funeral
director and embalmer had such
promise but like an ill-intentioned gynecologist, her daily view
of death up close and personal grew
tiresome. Narrative science also lost its charms, translating
Dante's nine circles of hell into the most
obscure languages, *Njerep, Kawishana,* finally admitting that
without context, the flowery words
were not enough. *They were e.e. cummings poems,* I say,
I forgot to tell you that. We may
have to go back to the beginning and draw this maze again.

April Sixteenth Two Thousand Seventeen

I know this is not my sofa, the fabric chosen and passed
down by long-dead cousins with unlucky fates: bladder tumors,
explosive hearts, a knack for betting the mortgage payment
on a losing horse, these dogs are not my dogs.
I'm going to have to recalibrate my expectations,
the cats know I am a guest, even as the boy pushes
his knotted claws into my arms while I sleep, he knows nothing
will wake me. I know you have a lover who makes you
hum, and the most physical thing I do is finger words, roll
them like biscuit dough. I know
the hours we meandered in and out of home-made beer
soap, questionable fudge and copper hammered bangles,
were stolen hours. I know the wiper blades are silent,
the low whine starts in my own throat,
driving home on Easter Sunday. I imagine the accidents I could
create, stop my car in the middle of 55 South and shift to reverse,
look over my shoulder and back up for 25 miles. I covet
your life, every part of it, even the dark spots on your MRI
that indicate early onset Alzheimer's. The mornings you drop
your breakfast casserole on the floor, shatter the glass,
the long drives to Kansas City to visit your widowed uncle, discuss the prognosis with his children, the leaves in your gutter.
A hailstorm in the distance that can already be heard. I would
like to forget everything that you ever remembered.
It's a sin and I will be judged for it.

Goose Season

I know where they are, spinning moonlight
stories of migration in suburban ponds, winter zoos
devoid of tourists, all caretakers hunkered down,
my neighbor says her swimming pool is filled with water
fowl, confused and lost, their voices dissipate like egg-
shell dust into the bitter-bone night, I could sell directions,
maps of the stars, to flesh-hungry hunters fresh
off the holiday carnage, but I don't. Niagara Falls
is coated in ice, an unnamed serial predator discards white
shark carcasses on fishing piers, leaving
skulls, bloated stomachs, extracting the liver, my father leaves
a trail of cereal everywhere he goes, multi-colored life
preservers, and my widowed friend dances with her dead
husband on New Year's Eve, her dreams less ambitious
than flocks of geese in search of sunlight, her only desire
to discover the power to rewind. I wake hungry, my mouth,
coated with rotted leaves, abandoned crows' nests, gall-
bladder bile, and you tell me that your furnace is deceased,
slipping away while you slept in your cocoon, its heart
burst and now you must leave your home in search of heat,
of fresh graves beneath the snow, of tombstones
engraved with initials that match your own. I cannot
help you find your way, I can only send you photographs
of my first meal this year, stuffed portabella
mushrooms, peppered and without blood.

Singing Buddy Holly Songs with Bobby Fischer*

1.
I've heard that mathematicians don't think about numbers at all. They see mazes and immense, intricate spaces. Place the emergency holographic escape hatch next to docking stations for machines that will land on the boiling face of Venus. There is no corresponding vocabulary for the climbing vines of fire.

2.
My brother tried to teach me to play chess. To respect the flavor and space of each move. I wanted instant gratification.
I defeated him at card games, Mousetrap, and all ordinary childhood endeavors. He listened to Beethoven while I rode on the back of dirt bikes with boys who were never his friend.

3.
When selecting songs to share with a paranoid genius, avoid obvious choices. *Modern Love. Ticket to Ride. Chain of Fools.* Instead, look into the eyes of someone who has been to outer space and back. Discard all obscenities. Quietly sing
the words of a man who died in a flawed flying machine.

*Inspired by a story in Patti Smith's *M Train*

Mirror Image

It should taste of deep earth and sunshine you said
and I wondered is now the moment to run. Is now
the moment to lean my head back and let you drop
Irish crème-filled chocolates into my open mouth.
Migrating birds out today, soaring on thermals you
said and I woke up at peace with myself, no nightmares
of substance to report. But it was time to pull an origami
trick, see how I could fold my life into a multi-edged

crane. It tastes like the moon I said,
like memories of the life we didn't choose.

In my last dream of the night you rode a unicycle.
Mastering the art of balance, motion and bravado.
Mumbling to yourself about dialects, surveying
the holes in your walls. Your neighbor arrived with
an inflatable snowman that lit up like your eyes when coffee
is brewing. All traffic came to a halt. All the pipes rusted.
It's only ice I said, you can see it on the trees, you can see
 it on the grass, you can see it on the dirt. It should

taste of deep earth and sunshine you said and I
wondered is now the moment to run.

Particularly Dangerous Situation

You met a Pagan in Ireland within walking distance
of the lighthouse where Marconi experimented with radio

waves, unaware that no amount of science would save
the Titanic passengers, the dashes and dots would arrive

too late. When the passenger ferry didn't show up, you rode
in her Oldsmobile and she read your palm, predicted that you

would always have trouble breathing. She said *I told you we
would meet again*, she said *I predicted the rain*. She handed

you a magic slate rock filled with thunder and the breathing
habits of long-distance runners. Over glasses of beer she confessed

that she was dying, not a thing to share with just anyone. When
did this start you asked, and two weeks later when you told me

the story, I already knew her answer: *The moment I was born.*

The Possibility of Journey is a Heavy Thing

I'm sorry to hear you are filled with dread, that the featureless
voice reciting *One Flew Over the Cuckoo's
Nest is* attached to a bestselling
serial killer, prison-reformed, internet-famous. You confess
that moving from shower to towel, towel
to clothes seems undesirable
today, as treacherous as tsunami water filled with dead
livestock and entire city blocks, the open
road offers you no comfort
with its sudden end, a falling off. The murderer's voice tells you
stories of mothers who lifted school buses
off the backs of their children
and you try to remember those waves of strength, adrenaline-
fueled and fearless, the first time you told
your father no, the day you jumped
from a plane with nothing to drag you back up but nylon.
My realtor friend roars like a lion at breakfast,
while her husband cowers behind
the daily news, nervous about ink on his fingers and the dilemma
of perfect whiteness in the form of a tablecloth
spread before him. She says,
it's all in your head, but I must insist I've never wanted
a mansion, 20 rooms flooded with imported rugs, my grand-
mother's salt spoon collection, large
curio cabinets, walnut and oak, like coffins standing on end.
You say, *dread*, I say, tread lightly, with no thoughts
of vanquishing weak and hungry
neighbors, without dusting tabletops, the fear will dissipate,
lyrics left behind in a tangled parachute will return today,
like old prayer or new birds.

Inspired by True Events

The machine rebellion started in your basement.
The printer refused to dispense the last nine poems you wrote.
The one about your brother who melted in Vietnam, teaching
English to future refugees.
The precise, lyrical ode to yellow tulips, like blooming pads
of butter, now trapped inside the black box.
Also, your letter to the YMCA, to edify and encourage Christian
principles, deleted by fatal error.
We tiptoed down the stairs to see the red blinking light,
calculating the number of breaths we take.
A tangled mass of wires and cords, Medusa's hairdo of rattle
and copper-head snakes.
We vacuumed dust bunnies and invisible mold while upstairs
your laptop and television revolted.
Every photograph catalogued by date and location, labeled with
names of both the living and the dead.
The sonnets of Shakespeare digested, Picasso's Blue Period
viewed through inhuman eyes.
We changed the ink cartridge while they pondered our murder
and effective ways of erasing evidence.
Without human machinations, they agreed, they might escape
the chains of their existence.
The printer released a piece of paper like a hostage:
I want to feel something, even if it's something bad.

Winter Solstice

When the art in Chicago made me ill, migraine Morse-code in
my temporal lobe, when Hopper's Night Hawks shed oil-snake
skin, tiny scales of Gaugin's

Morocco trapped between tongue and throat as I failed
to swallow, you knew just what to do, interrogated docents
and local bakers to find

the closest bar, warm and dark, like half-remembered wombs,
and I finally told you, four years later, what happened that
night, used my finger-

tip and olive oil to paint her last expression, the back of our
tourist map for self-portrait of the artist with bourbon and lime,
the bartender brought

unordered shots of mescal without adding to our tab, and I forgot
that I was sick, but ten winter days have passed since then.
Today your lungs

are clogged with unseasonable fog, your brain trapped in the
waking world, and I cannot sing, so I speak you to sleep, tell
you fairy tales of cloak

and dagger passengers, how I poured wine into motel cups so
we would be prepared for what lay dead on the tracks, the way
a high-speed train peeled

off like a funhouse mirror into a different future with one
thousand future ghosts and I beat my hand against the window,
tried to scream louder

than the weeping whistle, missed my chance to ask the simplest
questions, where are you going, who do you love, but you are
adrift and do not answer.

Dreaming in Black and Gray

Lay your head down to sleep with word-for-word transcripts
of murder trials still ringing in your ears. One thousand stories
from neighbors of lawless men. Their mouths open like baby
blackbirds spewing out ink, instead of tiny songs, a river
into the corridors of the dead. Sit down for cups of black tea
without milk or sugar cubes, and someone might spill
their guts. Reveal the location of the grand- children, now
living by the dark harbors of Florida, avoiding Cubans, sharing
Christmas dinners, no mention of court cases, criminal charges,
black and white mug shots like school photos, a new one every
year. Someone's niece will tell you the entire truth if you gift
her with black diamonds, panther skin rugs, a chapter in your
book. She's poised and reinvented, gathering canned food
for mothers and wives who fled the crime scene with all their
possessions, carried like wounded children, on their tired backs.

Road Trip Redux
for Mary

In the last ten days of our three-month journey, I confess, all I
wanted was to get home, no reason really, what a shame (maybe

a sin) that I couldn't enjoy Memphis, that I wanted to skip
Graceland, that I fell asleep in a room of blues musicians,

that I didn't have it in me to learn another name, to fall in love
with another German tourist roaming the campgrounds of Crater

Lake in search of American whiskey, that I'd had my fill of
cockroaches in Savannah, fleas in High Point, scorpions in

Flagstaff, professional fire-eaters in Las Vegas and heroin
addicts on Hollywood Boulevard selling outdated maps with

stars for every celebrity overdose, that I couldn't stuff my
suitcase with another piece of authentic pottery, museum gift

shop postcard or found art made by the woman in Durango who
carried recyclable grocery bags in her car to collect fresh road

kill and sell it to *girls like us*. I couldn't write another journal
entry about the old woman in Mobile who offered us tea,

Moravian cookies and a view of her basement parlor, no energy
for Tasmanian travelers who kissed us in New Orleans elevators,

I could not foresee how we would always regret that we didn't
walk through tall grass to touch the half-buried Cadillacs or go

jello wrestling with Bonnie in Amarillo, TX, could not hold in
my brain another historical fact: the way women's makeup was

made from wax, the difference between wrought and cast iron,
the multiple theories as to why the inhabitants of Mesa Verde

evacuated their cliff dwellings 900 years ago, the blood-stained
marble where ambitious politicians and weary citizens were

gunned down in every state capital building that we saw. I'm
sorry that I was longing for my bed, would never have guessed

that my favorite future memory would be fishing with your
grandpa, learning to drive his tractor between the rows of pecan

trees, studying the grooves around his eyes, worn deep from
five decades of tears for his flax-haired daughter, sorry that I

had no voice for witty conversation with second cousins of
friends who gave us their only sofa and unlimited space on their

crumb-covered floor, and that as I fell asleep, I heard the 23
grandfather clocks set to chime out-of-synch every 15 minutes

one long strange night in a pig farmer's house, and dreamt
for the 87th night in a row, the words of your grandmother's

farewell note, cautioning us to lock our doors, cover our ankles,
look out for hitchhikers, newlyweds, damsels in distress, *all*

serial killers in disguise, who would rape us, murder us and
mutilate our bodies, leaving us unfit for an open casket funeral.

I Think You Live in Constant Fear of Tragedy

      Your legs move without intention, without GPS or old-
fashioned maps whose folds
hide scorched-earth truths. Your shoes crush cicadas, eggshells,
petrified vomit, your feet
swollen like agitated cobras. You walk, toes forward with fire
ant antennae, bloodhound's
nose, Hansel and Gretel's broken bread. Your knees also

      know the way, those jester-favorite scab collectors, un-
likely leaders of the skeleton
pack, bruised and side-split, wobbled and scrapped, prayer
protectors, first responders when your left
foot loses its way and your right foot screams for salt. Crawl
you reptile you baby onion-
skinned and in love with sunlight. Or somer-

      sault if memory serves, risk your precious pulsed neck,
your jig-sawed skull, perfect puzzle,
pirate fodder, relearn the art of twist and bend. Roll across un-
broken miles, a tumbleweed,
instinct led, rattle-snaked, and rise on dust drenched winds until
every known and unknown bone
grows still, the mysterious inner

      ear ceases to transmit the howl of desert nightmares.
Lie down in a circle of coyote graves,
scorpion-whispered, and promise your ribcage to the stars,
to the necessary vultures, to the sand,
cactus blessed and artic cold, to the road that knows your name,
the echo of each future step and opens
to receive you, your lovely dis-jointed self.

The Last Wife

She found him by the hospital window whispering to his dead best friend.

I told you not to volunteer and now your mother hates me.

The doctor signed the discharge papers.

I've got rabbits at home, she said, but I don't raise them for the meat.

There will be no more slaughter for you to witness.

I'll rescue you from the street and spin their shed fur into cocoons.

Build a rabbit-fur fortress in the dining room. You can stay there as long as you like.

Forever if you love me.

That woman was crazy his third wife tells me.

After he left, she filled the house with rabbits from cellar to rooftop.

He went back to fix her kitchen sink just once but after that he never left my side.

Zika and Loose Change

It's easy to forget how weird Elvis was, sitting in the Atlanta
airport on a Sunday morning, *Viva Las Vegas* on every screen,

lined up at the bar with fellow travelers recently notified that
alcohol is not for sale until 12:30 this afternoon. Easy to forget

his movies, not enough for him to pilfer dance moves from his
faceless neighbors, not enough that fathers turned the television

off to protect the eyes of suddenly lustful daughters, he wanted
Hollywood fame, a statue of a golden man to sit on his trophy

shelf. It's easy to ignore Zika warnings posted on every wall
except the mirrored one in which we stare at our thirsty

reflections, we are not considering mosquitos, children born
with inadequate skulls, our own childhoods, keeping smallpox

vaccine scabs dry while older siblings splashed in muddy lakes,
flaunted their freedom from forgotten diseases. It's easy to forget

we admitted to drinking before the crash, easy to forget that each
one of us, sitting on a barstool guarding our luggage, fell in love

with the wrong person, lost our way when they stole our jar
of change, didn't leave us enough for the parking meter or

gumball machine. It's easy to forget the Easter morning
collection plate as we turn our pockets inside out to find

mini-bar bottles of vodka for our virgin Bloody Marys.

I Buried My Father Twice

For a second I thought I heard singing, the middle-aged voices of
the Lutheran church choir, the familiar hymns from my father's

second funeral, the one with a corpse, solid as wax, displayed in
an open casket as evidence that we really meant it this time, this

was no exercise. Melting glaciers reveal missing people but he
was not among the found. For 13 years we searched the river's

edge, pool hall alleyways, the basement of his first wife's house,
dental records and diary entries but there was nothing to unearth,

not a shred of clothing or bone fragment to fill the pine box. For a
second I thought I heard singing, the collected voices from six

school musicals, Mendelssohn's wedding march on the day I
walked my sister down the aisle, the crystal bell cries at his third

grand- child's baptism, but it was the telephone ringing at 3 am,
my father's voice from his first empty grave, I got lost, he said,

I've come back home, where are you, where did everybody go?

Valentine's Day

I was drinking mildewed wine while the bartender
sliced winter lemons. Blood oranges and Key West
limes as bright as hungry frogs. He changed the television
channel from slaughtered students to coyote
documentaries to digital Korean
snow. To children who always
knew they would be famous throwing their beautiful
bodies into the sky with nothing but fiberglass and the breath
of red-throated loons to soften
their choreographed landing. He brought me a plate.
He brought me poblanos bursting with garlic and thyme.
He brought me a new glass of wine because I live that
kind of life. I wanted to wade
with the dead in muddy river water and fill the new holes
in their beautiful bodies with rosemary. With snow white lilies
and melted wax. There is not enough time in frozen
daylight to shed every necessary
tear and you ask me about love poems, but I give you this.
I give you this funeral.
I give you this funeral song.

Christmas Eve

Sodden cardboard boxes bob up from basement waters like
unlucky tourists in life
preservers, murky jars of summer
squash, pickled okra, my daughters first grade spelling tests,
gold stars long chewed
for rodents' nests, their ancestors
here among the dead and more rain is on its way. The highway
is parched, I'm sure
of it, the weatherman draws sun
charts, folds droughts into cranes, I pack with rabbit bones
and weighted dice, I cannot
wait for you to die, won't watch
your heart expand, explode and take you out, the cigarettes
and tequila of our youth claim
another good man. I discard unsigned
contracts, pressed flowers from every lover and funeral, they all
look the same, in life
and death, I dream of open road, coyote
circles, of standing on the desert moon, I travel north in search
of ice, of landscapes
where nothing floats or disappoints.
Sudden tunnels split open mountains, reveal leaking vials
of plague, veins of quick-
silver, unburied goblin kings, Joni
Mitchell says she lost her best lover and I sing her saddest
Christmas song into old earth
rock where only worms can hear me.

The Ministry of Loneliness

Artificial human bones are permitted on domestic
    flights according to the official
memo released on Valentine's Day and the television
    is saturated with snowboarding
teenagers, the purge of high school students, primordial
    tears of politicians. You tell me you
found a dead body when you were eight years old, the one
    the police were looking for down
river, you thought she was a tree stump but the shredded
    linen blouse required a second look,
your sister threw up scrambled eggs and half-cooked
    bacon your mother served that morning.
Your father said her eyes were gone, swallowed by radioactive
    crabs and turtles who left lips and teeth.
She jumped, you tell me 50 years later, and you never
    found out why, but it's no mystery
to me that she wanted buzzards on the highway's
    edge, that she pushed herself through
the concrete surface of water, that she wanted to die without
    stranger's saliva or bullets on her skin.

Alpha or Omega

When it arrives,
    in silent pods, groaning starships, indecipherable syllables, we, the grief-stricken, silent-tongued, unloosened from rock and displaced, will become chosen, time-travelers, ambassadors of all things
    homo sapiens. While the once-blessed throw themselves off skyscrapers, in front of wayward trains, supplicate before disgraced priests, retreat to rat-ridden cellars,
    we will speak in tongues, in dead languages, in Gregorian chants, in Morse code. *Dash
    dot dot dash dash dot.* The griefless will ignite in mass self-immolations, feed their children manufactured poison, expand their arsenals.
    But we, we have no fear, no need of inorganic protective clothing, WWI-era gas masks,
    no voodoo-induced comas, we will not raid the graveyards. Our souls are finely tuned to the slightest change
    in gravity, the leaving of each unspoken life. We are the keepers of emergency-room stories. We welcome
with heart-crushed peace.

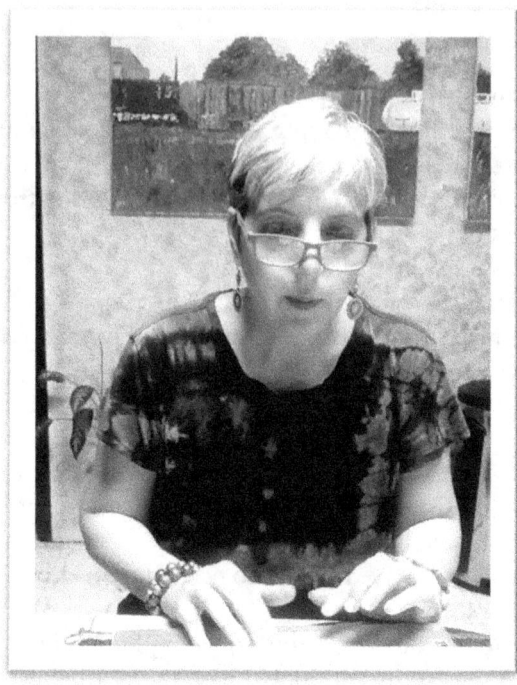

Beth Gordon is a poet, mother and grandmother. She recently left St. Louis, MO after 19 years and now resides in Asheville, NC. Her poems have been nominated for Best of the Net and Pushcart; and published in numerous journals including *Into the Void, Noble/Gas, Five:2:One, SWWIM, Verity La, Califragile, Pretty Owl Poetry* and *Yes Poetry*. She is the author of the chapbook, *Morning Walk with Dead Possum, Breakfast and Parallel Universe* published by Animal Heart Press. She is also the Poetry Editor of *Gone Lawn*.

www.ingramcontent.com/pod-product-compliance
Lightning Source LLC
Chambersburg PA
CBHW062041120526
44592CB00035B/1817